THE TREMENDOUS TREE BOOK

THE TREMENDOUS TREE BOOK

by Barbara Brenner and May Garelick

illustrated by Fred Brenner

Boyds Mills Press

Published by
Caroline House
Boyds Mills Press, Inc.
A Highlights Company
815 Church Street
Honesdale, Pennsylvania 18431
Printed in Hong Kong

Originally published by Four Winds Press, A Division of Scholastic
Magazines, Inc., New York, NY

Publisher Cataloging-in-Publication Data

Brenner, Barbara.
          The tremendous tree book / by Barbara Brenner and May Garelick; illustrated
by Fred Brenner
40p. :col. ill. ; cm.
Originally published by Four Winds Press, New York, 1979.
Summary: Told in simple rhyme, these verses celebrate the marvels of trees.
Cut-paper illustrations supplement the text.
Hardcover ISBN 1-878093-56-8   Paperback ISBN 1-56397-718-4
1. Trees--Juvenile literature. [1. Trees.] I. Garelick, May, joint author. II. Brenner, Fred,
ill. III. Title.
582/.16--dc20   [E]   1998
Library of Congress Catalog Card Number: 91-73753

Hardcover 10 9 8 7 6 5 4 3 2

Paperback 10 9 8 7 6 5 4 3 2 1

LIVING TREE

A tree is a plant.

A plant with a woody stem

That almost always grows tall.

All trees are plants.

But not all plants
are trees.

TELL A TREE

One tree.

Another tree.

Lots of different trees.

Different shapes.

Different bark.

Different blossoms.

Different fruit.

Different leaves.

That's how you tell one tree
from another.

And that's
a fact.

LODGEPOLE PINE

JAMAICA PALM

NORTHERN RED OAK

SUGAR MAPLE

TREE LEAVES

The easiest way to tell a tree is by its leaves.
Each kind of tree has
its own kind of leaf.
No two leaves are ever exactly alike —
even on the same tree.

Pine needles are
leaves, too.
A big pine tree can have
20 million leaves.

MESQUITE

YELLOW POPLAR

EASTERN HOP HORNBEAM

INCENSE CEDAR

PLAINS COTTONWOOD

AMERICAN HOLLY

COMMON HOPTREE

AMERICAN ELM

WHITE ASH

TREE GAME

Here's a leaf matching game.
Pick a leaf from several different trees
in your neighborhood.
See how many of your leaves
match the ones on these pages.

PAPER BIRCH

SWEETGUM

QUAKING ASPEN

TREE FOOD

A tree makes food
in its leaves.
Sunbeams shine on green leaves,
mix with air and water
and make sugar.
A tree makes food for itself
as long as its leaves are green.

Plants are the only things
in the whole world
that make their own food.

That's what they call
pho-to-syn-the-sis.

TREE HISTORY

There had to be plants on earth
before there could be animals.
There were trees
before there were dinosaurs,
or insects.
Even before grass.
Trees have lived and died here
for about 300 million years.

A tree keeps on growing
for as long as it lives.
There's a bristlecone pine in Nevada
that's about 4,900 years old.

It's the oldest living tree.

TREE GIANTS

The biggest trees in the world
are the giant Sequoias.
There is one that weighs 2,000 tons —
as much as 66 blue whales.
There's enough wood in that tree
to make 40 houses.
Twelve people standing with their arms outstretched
can't reach all the way around its trunk.

TREE MIDGETS

The smallest trees in the world
are the Arctic birches.
They almost never get to be
more than 10 inches high.

Look at me,
I'm taller
than a tree.

SAFE TREE

Someone's on this branch.

And that one.

And that one.

Trees give animals a place to nest.

And roost.

And rest.

TREE HOLE

A hole in a tree
is usually home
for something.
A wet hole is a tiny pond —
a place for mosquitoes,
tree frogs,
or polliwogs.

A dry hole can be
a woodpecker's nest,
a bee's hive,
an owl's place . . .

Or a raccoon's
den!

TREE SEEDS

What makes trees?
Trees make trees —
by dropping seeds.
Nut seeds. Fruit seeds.
Round seeds. Flat ones.
Seeds with wings and parachutes.
Pop! Witch hazel seeds open with a bang.

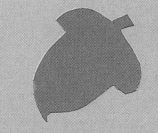

Inside each seed is everything
that's needed to make a tree.
Some seeds get eaten by animals and birds.
Others fall to the ground,
get buried in the soil,
and grow.

Look for baby trees
under big trees.

ACORN TREE

Acorns are the seeds of oak trees.
One oak tree can make 5,000 acorns
in a season.
When acorns drop, acorn eaters come . . .
Bears. Deer. Porcupines. Chipmunks.
Lots of animals feed on acorns.

Squirrels and raccoons too!

Not all acorns get eaten.
Some of them grow into oak trees.
If there were no acorns
there could be no oak trees.
No oak trees, no acorns.

No acorns,
poor squirrels!

FOREST TREES

Lots of seeds make lots of trees.
Lots of trees make a forest.
Forests are cool.
Some hot day, stand under a tree
in a forest.
Feel how cool it is.
The leaves give off water.
The water cools the air.
The branches make shade.
One big tree can have the cooling power
of 100 air conditioners.

FOOD TREE

These are the leaves of the wild cherry tree.
This is the caterpillar that eats
the leaves of the wild cherry tree.
This is the shrew that eats the caterpillar
that eats the leaves.
And this is the owl that eats the shrew
that eats the caterpillar
that eats the leaves
of the wild cherry tree.
Trees are food for many creatures.

TREE TREATS

Cherries. Pick the fruit. Make a pie.

Oranges. Peel one and eat it.

Tap the sap of the sugar maple. Make syrup.

Apples for cider. Squeeze out the juice.

Use lemons for lemonade,

make limeade from limes.

Crack a coconut from

the coconut palm.

Drink the milk.

TREE THINGS

Trees make more than 5,000 different things used by people.

Even this book is made from trees.

Plant a tree.
Squirrels do.

TREE COLOR

Autumn.

Some trees turn color

and begin to drop their leaves.

Leaves pile up on the ground.

The clean-up squad comes.

They chew, grind, and break up the dead leaves.

Ground up leaves make soil.

Soil is food for plants.

They're called evergreens.

TREE SOIL

Want to see a clean-up squad?

Take an old sheet.

Put it under a tree.

Put stones at the corners to hold it down.

Come back in a week.

Scoop up a handful of leaves.

You'll see grubs, worms, millipedes

and other tiny creatures

that turn dead, brown leaves into soil.

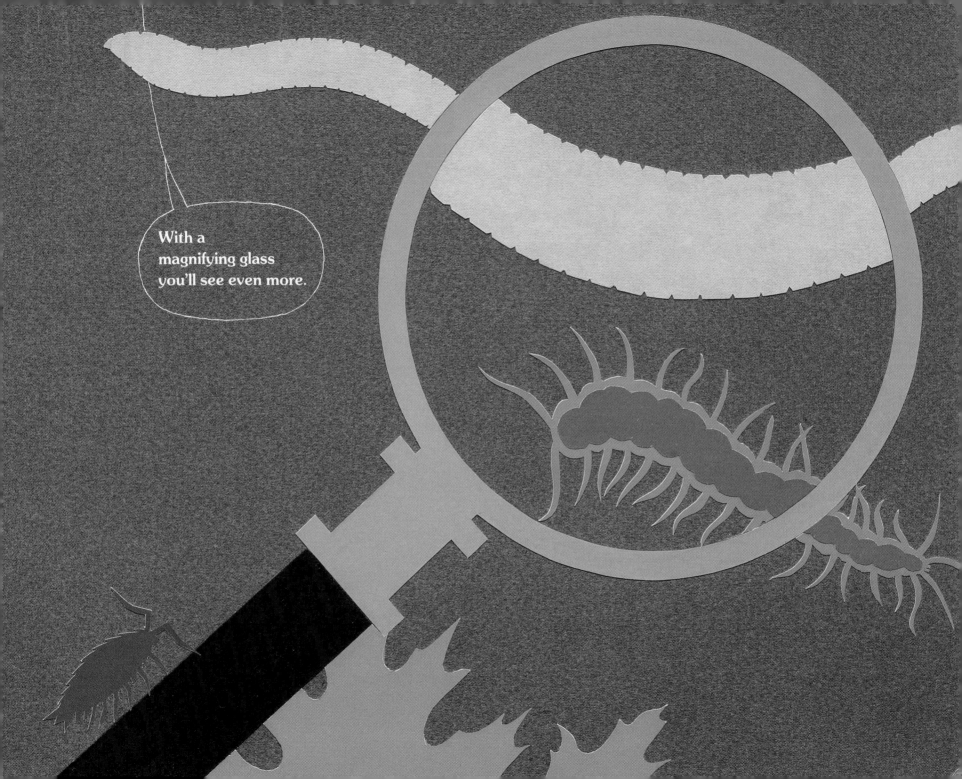

CHANGING TREE

No leaves.
The tree looks dead.
But —
next year's leaves and blossoms
are already there. Where?

Folded up inside each bud,
waiting for warm weather.
Watch how the leaf buds
open all together one spring day.
Watch the tree come alive.

COUNTING-OUT RHYME

by Edna St. Vincent Millay

Silver bark of beech, and sallow
Bark of yellow birch and yellow
  Twig of willow.
Stripe of green in moosewood maple,
Color seen in leaf of apple,
  Bark of popple.
Wood of popple pale as moonbeam
Wood of oak for yoke and barn-beam,
  Wood of hornbeam.
Silver bark of beech, and hollow
Stem of elder, tall and yellow
  Twig of willow.